TITHING REMOVES *the* CURSE *of* POVERTY

CAROLYN WEBB

WESTBOW
PRESS®
A DIVISION OF THOMAS NELSON
& ZONDERVAN

WestBow Press books may be ordered through booksellers or by contacting:

WestBow Press
A Division of Thomas Nelson & Zondervan
1663 Liberty Drive
Bloomington, IN 47403
www.westbowpress.com
1 (866) 928-1240

ISBN: 978-1-9736-9396-3 (sc)
ISBN: 978-1-9736-9395-6 (hc)
ISBN: 978-1-9736-9397-0 (e)

Library of Congress Control Number: 2020910540

Print information available on the last page.

WestBow Press rev. date: 6/24/2020

They stole my Heart

Special thanks to my Munchkins

Tamara, Toniesha, Joe, Celeste

In Loving Memory of

Kimberli Marie Taper

CONTENTS

INTRODUCTION

Removing the Curse of Poverty *is my dream to educate, elevate, and illuminate the connection of your finances to the word of God. My goal is to share some of my personal experiences and tools that will help you to control the flow of cash, get out of debt, and thus remove the curse of poverty in your life. The Biblical Principle of Sowing and Reaping will elevate you to a new dimension of expectancy based upon what God has promised in his word. Being fruitful and multiplying! Leaving a Legacy!*

Yes, I believe there is a direct relationship between our spiritual life and money. A good steward consults God in all matters of life to receive divine direction, especially matters of money. I believe we should always share the wisdom of our experiences. Train our children through the wisdom of our experiences. Teach our children the wisdom of becoming a good steward.

When I think of Poverty, various terms come to mind, such as ownership, stewardship, responsibility, and accountability.

I hope to share my perspective regarding these terms using the word of God. Managing spiritual wealth (relationship with God) determines how much God can trust us with worldly blessings (money). God loves a cheerful giver. When we sow sparingly, we also reap sparingly. When we sow generously, we reap generously. Reaping and Sowing is a principle that touches all aspects of life. Therefore, what you need more of; you give more of that thing away! Exceedingly and abundantly, above all you could ask or think, according to the power that works within us.

(Ephesians 3:20 KJV)

God's word offers Hope and Promise via our pipeline to him through prayer. The word comes alive when we hear it, when we speak it, and when we apply it.

"Remember, a closed mouth can't be fed; neither can a closed hand receive!"

We must go to the root of a thing where it begins and dissect it.

(Proverbs 23:7 KJV) *tells us that so as a man thinks in his heart, so is he! This scripture challenges us to examine what is going on in our hearts.*

(Romans 12:2 KJV) *directs us to transform our thinking by the renewing of our minds!*

What are your thoughts regarding money? How do you feel about money in your spirit? Are you responsible with money?

This is not a get rich quick scheme, or seven steps to prosperity. I realized poverty involved more than money, but my mind and my heart as well. I explored three components of poverty and addressed them in my life. It is my personal journey utilizing the bible as my weapon to curse poverty from my mind, my heart, and lastly my finances.

I offer tools that are aimed to make you a better steward over all aspects of your life. ***Real Life tools for Real Life Issues!***

TITHING REMOVES THE CURSE OF POVERTY

PART ONE

CHANGE YOUR MIND

Journey with me as I build the foundation that Changed My Mind!

<u>Ownership</u>

For believers, life did not happen by osmosis or a big bang! All our senses; the capacity to see, touch, taste, feel comes from God. The ability to obtain wealth also comes from God. God owns everything, including us! ***(Psalms 24:1 KJV)*** *tells us "the earth is the Lord's and the fullness thereof, and all of us who live on the earth.*

Now ... since God owns everything, that would make us stewards, managers, administrators over the things we are responsible for and the people we are responsible to. A good steward, manager, administrator desires to keep the boss happy and in obedience commits themselves and their possessions to God. God has the *ownership rights to everything. Remember, it is God who gives us the ability to obtain wealth. (***Deuteronomy 8:18 (KJV)*** Those boss dreams, ideas, gifts, and talents we have, all come from God.*

<u>Responsibility</u>

Stewards have the responsibility of managing. A good Steward can manage family, their time, his or her talent and his or her tenths. We are responsible for the gifts, talents and financial opportunities given to us. What do we own that God did not give to us? I know, I know, the first thought that used to come to my mind was "I worked and hustled for mine." Well, yes, I did, I worked and hustled with the ability that God gave to me. Have you ever wondered how two people with the same skills and opportunities arrive with different results? We shall address that in depth in accountability.

*We personally own nothing, even the very air we breathe. We are mere stewards with responsibility over what we have. God richly gives us everything and therefore he owns everything. (**Luke 10:27 KJV**) tells us to love God with all our hearts and love our neighbors as ourselves. So, we are even held responsible on how we are to **LOVE**!*

Part One: ***What is on Your Mind***

Accountability

We are all accountable for our gifts, talents, and opportunities given to us as stewards.

(Matthew 25:14-40 KJV) *the* ***Parable of the Talents****. It gave me Spiritual insight on how God viewed my stewardship over money. I love this story, so I paraphrase:*

A man with three servants went on an extended trip. He gave the first servant, 5 talents; he gives the second servant, 2 talents; and gives 1 talent to the third servant. The bible said he gave to each ***in accordance to his ability. Did you get that? God does not give us anything we are not able to handle. God will never give us an assignment that he will not enable us to complete.***

This was so powerful to me*, so let me break this down in my mind; those things you and I do well, God gave us the ability to do it. The scripture brings into play,* ***Purpose****! You and I excel in,* ***purposed ability!*** *We only get what we can handle!* ***Purpose!*** *I only get what I can handle. So, there is no need to be intimidated or covet another's talents or skills, because you have talents and skills of your own! We are not all athletes, or actors,* *or singers, but we can excel in the talents and skills given to us. Time is wasted coveting the gifts of others when you can use that energy to explore your very own gifts and talents. I encourage you to focus and enhance the skills and talents given to you because the scripture says you have the* ***purposed ability****.*

Our mind is complexed and intricately interwoven with feelings, perceptions, our wills, intellect and reasoning. Our minds take directions from our hearts. The mind is a scheming tool used to solve problems. Depending upon how we feel or perceive a person, place, or thing, we form thoughts and opinions from those feelings. The mind then produces and or executes what is in our hearts. The mind and heart works hand in hand. Our hearts reveal who we really are!

(Jeremiah17:9 KJV) tells us that our hearts are deceitful above all things and desperately wicked. Who can know it?

REMOVING THE CURSE OF POVERTY

Part One: ***What is on Your Mind***

The first servant invested and doubled the talent. He invested according to the ***ability*** *given him and turned (profited) the five talents into ten. The second servant also invested and doubled (profited) his talent. I am of the conclusion the first and second* *servants were gifted in the understanding of money management. The first two servants activated the ability which God gave to them.*

*The third servant created a story in his mind based upon the feelings in his heart regarding the man. (**Matthew 25: 24-25**) The third servant played it safe and buried the one talent. The third servant wanted to absolve himself of any **responsibility**, so he hid his talent in the ground.*

The Hebrew word for heart is "Lebab" and the Greek word for mind is "Kardin". I mentioned these so we can understand the hidden things we hide in our hearts, way down in our inner self. (ego) It is down in our inner self that we exercise faith, it is where our wisdom is employed. Although understanding is a function of the mind; the heart is where we discern between right and wrong, so the connection is undeniable.

Emotional Intelligence Consultant, DB Bedford's secret #15 emotional storyboarding. *The third servant created a story in his mind regarding the man to avoid accountability. We often create stories in our mind based upon our lack of understanding regarding a person, place, or thing. We also come to a biased conclusion based upon the story we've created. The heart highlights the emotions and our mind responds to those* *feelings in actions. It is difficult to see a picture if you are sitting inside of the frame. I have this weakness for my daughters where I purposely pray and ask God* ***when*** *and* ***if*** *I should intervene to their needs. My emotions battle with my mind because I do not want them to depend more upon me than they depend upon* ***God.*** *This is tricky because I do not want to play God in their lives! If they are* ***not*** *good Stewards over what they now have, they will not be able to handle the blessings God has in store for their future. Everyone needs their own personal relationship with God! Everyone will be held accountable on how you handled what you are given.*

The decisions we make regarding money starts in the mind; the danger shows up when we add our emotions. Financial decisions made through emotions, is a recipe for disaster.

***<u>Part One:</u>* What is on Your Mind**

After a long time, the ***Man*** *returned. He went to the first servant to account his five talents. The first servant said" Master you have entrusted me with five talents, and I have gained you five more. The* ***Man*** *replied, "Well done thy good and faithful servant". You have been faithful over a few things. I will make you ruler over many! Come and share in your master's happiness.*

The ***Man*** *went to the servant with two talents who also doubled his investment and gained two more. The second servant also heard "Well done thy good and faithful servant" You have been faithful over a few things. I will make you ruler over many! Come and share in your master's happiness.*

The third servant created a story in his heart based upon feelings. The servant told himself the Master was a harsh man, so he was afraid. He buried the talent, in hopes that would end his responsibility and he would no-longer be held accountable. The third servant failed to use the talent given to him and thus lost his reward. He acted upon the story created in his heart. ***(Matthew 25:28-30 KJV)*** *He did not try.*

We may not conquer or accomplish everything we attempt, but we can at least try!

Webster's Dictionary describes Poverty as the state of being poor; the condition of being without adequate food, money or shelter. Poverty is the state of having little or no money, goods or means of support. Poverty is limited resources to meet ones needs. The third servant displayed poor thinking that was rooted in his heart. The state of the third servants mind was restricting and limiting, yet under his control. The circumstance of poverty is a condition which makes an imprint on our minds, yet we still have control over the actions we take.

My New definition for Poverty *is a temporary state we will not allow to take up space in our thought process, our spirit, emotions, or finances. Poverty is a curse which can be addressed by obedience to the word of God.* ***I Declare and Believe*** *the curse of poverty ends now in your life and (we) commit to utilizing what we presently have combined with the word of God, to change our circumstances****. In Jesus Name! AMEN****.*

*The lack of money creates an atmosphere for poverty when our ideal conflicts with our reality. Poverty then seeps into our mind set. So, let us begin with identifying poor thinking habits. Removing the Curse of Poverty will not make you a millionaire unless you choose to do the work and become one. Removing the curse of Poverty will free your mind and spirit regarding money. I began my journey simply being obedient in paying the Lord's Tithe as instructed in (****Malachi 3. KJV***

I accepted God as my Lord and Savior at an incredibly early age; however, I did not come into a full understanding of the finance connection until I became a young adult. I learned early in life that I was a giver, even if it was only a word of encouragement. It was all a part of my purpose! My assignment as care giver was ad lib for family members. My advisement on how to handle money was all done prior to any formal education. It came so easy and comfortable, I thought why not understand how God views money, he owns it all. My understanding of what I learned brought me to the place I am today. I began to tithe a dime on a dollar, the more I gave, the more knowledge I gained. I was blessed to understand the significance of ***(Malachi 3. KJV)*** *God* ***did*** *open those windows of heaven in my life.*

To this day he continues to bless me and rebuke that devourer, so I can bless someone else. I was blessed to understand the intangibles, things money cannot buy! ***Obeying the word of God removes curses.*** *When I, we, you, obey the word of God,* ***it removes curses****! There is no other entity in heaven or on this earth that can interrupt God's power and authority in your life!*

Yes, I believe there is a direct relationship in how we think, what is in our spirit and how it appears in our management of money. The three components of poverty must align with the word of God. Possessing money does not make you wealthy or rich. We will discuss later how illness has no respect of money. The first principle component was my belief system or mindset.

(Hebrews 11:6 KJV) *speaks to* ***Faith*** *and tell us that without faith it is impossible to please God, because anyone who comes* *to him (GOD) must believe **he exist** and the he (GOD)is a **rewarder** of those **who diligently seek him**.*

*It had to be a part of my psyche to believe the earth is the Lord's and the fullness thereof, the world and all that dwell therein. **(Psalms 24:1 KJV)** This includes you, you, and me! It was impossible to claim the title of being a good steward until my mind was convinced that God owns **EVERYTHING!***

I Changed my Mind!

WATCH

Watch your thoughts; they become words. Watch your words; they become actions.

Watch your actions; they become habits. Watch your habits; they become character.

Watch your character; it affects the destiny of your purpose. (unknown)

(Genesis, chapters 1-7 KJV)** gives us detailed breakdown of how God spoke the world into existence. **"Let there be"** <u>**it was, and it still is."**</u> The moon, stars, sun, he spoke them into existence. God spoke it and it was done. He commanded it and what he spoke into existence stills stands fast. **(Psalms 33:9

KJV) *We take our cars back to the dealership when it needs maintenance. Why? We feel the dealer is skilled in the mechanics of the vehicle. We visit the doctor when there is some dis-ease in our bodies because we acknowledge the doctor went to medical school and is knowledgeable in his craft. So, in turn, we should go to God with all our issues because he created us in our mother's womb. He cares for us and tells us to cast our cares upon him because* ***HE Cares for US!***

(Genesis 1:27 KJV) God created us in his own image*. We are fearfully and wonderfully made, a little lower than the angels in the hierarchy of things. God chose to get up close and personal when he created man. God formed man out the dust of the ground. God breathed the breathe life into man's nostrils and man became a living soul. Humans are housed with multiple, intricate systems at work within us; digestive system, skeletal system, nervous system, respiratory, major and minor organs just to name a few. Were created and designed with a* ***divine purpose****.*

In the center of our soul is a huge void only God can fill*. Our hearts enable us to love and experience God on a spiritually intimate basis. We are so connected to him that without him we can do absolutely nothing. Without a relationship with God, we are always in search of someone or something to fill that* *void. When my mind is in turmoil, I look to the* ***word for instruction****. When my souls cry out, I seek the* ***comfort of his word*** *as I talk to God in prayer. Housed in the word of God is* ***restoration and recovery****. The Word is our* ***lifeline****. I will forever be a student of the Word of God!*

Most have lived in survival mode all our lives because survival was all we knew. Our parents were financially savvy in making things stretch and doing the best they could with what they had. I am thankful for my parents who unknowingly dropped the spirit of hustle (determination) on me. We each are the result of our socialization. We were either born into poor situations, forced into poor situations, or experienced poor opportunities. Well, I offer a different perspective. Now that I know who truly owns everything, then I know to depend on him for all things. We are blessed through the promises God has given us in his word.

God's invests in people! *Money is simply one of the tools he uses to enhance his investments. That would be* ***US!*** *If you have not incorporated helping, assisting, or investing in the welfare of human beings, what are you doing? When you pour into another human being, you sharpen your skills and enrich their lives as well. Reaching out to others comes back to us. Each one Teach One! Loving your neighbor as yourself, reciprocates on all cylinders. The circle of life for humans; is* ***Humans****! Loving,* *supporting, and encouraging each other costs nothing and gives great dividends.*

I began to apply scripture to every aspect of my life. I then learned the true meaning of sowing and reaping, reciprocity. ***(Malachi KJV)*** *says when I am a good steward over the finances God blessed me with, I am no longer cursed but blessed. Ten percent of my time, talent, and finances put me directly under that window God would open and pour me out a blessing. I would not be able to contain. In the beginning, it was only my time and talent because I was not born with the proverbial silver spoon in my mouth. Money was coming in, yet I was not making good financial decisions. I saw it, and I bought it, point blank and the period.* ***Survival Mode!***

The third servant in the parable of the talents also operated in survival mode. The third servant did not ***place value*** *on the opportunity given to him so he played it safe, nothing ventured and nothing gained, We all have not capitalized or not valued an opportunity at one time or another simply due to the lack of wisdom, understanding, and trust.*

People, reaping and sowing is real! *When I sowed sparingly, I reaped sparingly. When I criticized others, I was criticized. When I gossiped about others, I was gossiped about as well.*

Whatever I released into this universe good, bad, or indifferent, it returned to me. Whatever you release into the atmosphere will return to you! It is so easy to critique others rather than looking at ourselves in the mirror. It is a scary thought looking at ourselves, but it is a must to see who we really are.

Recently, I experienced a lack of communication on a credit union account. I accused the credit union in my mind, heart and body posture of money not credited to my account. I later found out that I had deposited the money into another account. I became extremely anxious and annoyed with the situation to the point of mentally and emotionally shutting down. I closed the account. My daughter said to me, "Mother I've never seen you obsess over money before." I stood looking at this voice of reason and thinking wow, reality check. I had to apologize to the teller because she was pleading to show me the camera footage. The windows of my mind had bars on it. Of course, I felt I right, what else could it have been? The stories we tell ourselves!

My daughter watched the transaction on camera because my emotions were at an all- time high, and my logic was non-existent. More important than the money was ***my need to be right****. Although I did not speak verbally, my body language spoke volumes of my arrogance. Once outside of the frame, I could see the picture so clearly of myself having an* ***adult temper***

***tantrum**. I am sharing this to alert some and warn others not to be **controlled** or **obsessed** by money. I am meticulously passionate about money which made it imperative that I changed my mind on how I viewed money. My brand-new attitude did not match the blessings God continuously gives to me. I humbled myself and I apologized to the teller. My maturity and ability to handle money came into question. How can I teach my daughters and others about money and not control my own emotions? Obsession is not a lesson I wish to leave them. I constantly remind myself from where I started. So, I purposely operate through humility even when it is **uncomfortable.** The customer (**me**) is **NOT** always right. Yes, Christians strive to be Christ-like, but we are not perfect. I say this in defense of the holier than thou jacket that is often-times placed on Christians. We are human too!*

*I am visual in my understanding, so the word of God always paints the picture for me. Once I am blessed to understand something, **I GOT IT!** I can vividly remember a time when I was on welfare. I thank God for welfare and the ability to utilize it as a training tool. I thank God for all the working citizens who paid and pay into the welfare system. I am thankful to pay into this system myself. I can identify! Welfare gave me on the job skills in surviving off a little while attending college. I will never forget asking my daughter to go to the corner store to purchase a loaf* *of bread. I tried to hand my daughter the book of food stamps only to turn and see her face flooded with tears. My daughter said to me* ***"I did not know we were poor."*** *I fought back the laughter. I did not see myself as poor, but my daughter associated food stamps with poverty. I am a realist! I saw food stamps as putting food in our mouths! I also remember our house burning down and having to go to the Red Cross. The Red Cross offered some type of food voucher,* ***which I accepted****!*

My husband instructed me to give them back, but once again, I saw those vouchers as food on the table. I am still grateful to this day for those food stamps and the food voucher. I saw those food stamps as a part of the journey to my purpose. Food Stamps were a temporary part of reality at that time of my life. ***NOT*** *a permanent fixture!* ***(Proverbs 16:1 KJV)****, says pride before destruction and a hearty spirit before a fall. Our paychecks were burning with everything else inside that house.* ***(No Direct Deposit in those days)*** *These stories help keep me grounded, thankful, and humbled.*

(Isaiah 55:11 KJV) says God's word does not return to him void but accomplishes what it was sent out to do! *This speaks volumes to me. My take way from this scripture is when I align my belief system up with the word of God, things begin to happen, my needs, wants and desires begin to manifest* *themselves. My obedience opened a door, then another door, then another door and so on!*

*I began tithing ten percent of my gross income or first increase which belongs to God. Why does it belong to him? It is God who gives us the ability to gain wealth and in obedience to the word in (**Malachi 3:8-12 KJV**)*

*Paraphrased, asks will a man rob God? The reply was how? God said with tithes and offering you have withheld and now the **entire nation is cursed with a curse**.*

*God says to; bring all the tithes into the storehouse, so there may be food in my house; tell us to try him, test and see if he does not open up the windows of heaven and pour us out blessings that we won't have room enough to receive. God goes on to say he will rebuke the devourer for our sake and nations will call us blessed. My takeaway from **Malachi 3** God owns everything, so he does not **NEED** our money, but he desires our **Obedience**.*

*There was a time Uncle Sam had his hands so deep in my pockets until I began to believe I was exclusively working for him. Uncle Sam did not ask my permission, he did not buy me flowers, candy, or anything! Basically, you earn a certain amount of money; you pay a certain amount of taxes. When you earn money, **you will pay taxes,** the law of the land.*

***<u>Malachi 3</u>**: God is speaking overflow, not having room enough to receive, so I incorporated the principle of tithing and made a **financial covenant with God**. God directed my finances and I humbly, thankfully, and cheerfully pay the Lord's tithe. Things started to change right before my eyes. Minister Jeffrey Williams exhorted about how God suddenly answers our prayers oftentimes before we get them out of our mouths. I found myself trying to explain it through some mathematical equation, but the equation could not address the overflow. I began to see such overflow in my life until I had to double check to make sure I had paid everything. Some bills were paid in advance.*

*My goal is to bless my church and leave a legacy for my children; grand; and great grandchildren. I **changed my mind and my speech**. I challenge you to change your language (**the words you speak over yourselves**) it will then change your mind (**how you perceive yourself**) **When you change your mind; you then change <u>your atmosphere</u> which changes your outcome!***

(Proverbs 18:21**KJV**) tell us Death and Life is in the Power of the tongue, and they that love it shall eat the fruit thereof. SO! … SPEAK LIFE!

As my faith increased, my impact increased, and the Lord's Tithe increased. You CAN live an abundant life in real-time … OVERFLOW!

Restoration Mentality

> *"I will restore to you the years that the swarming locust has eaten …" Joel 2:25*
>
> *We serve a God of restoration! You may have had some disappointments or unfair things Happen in your life; but instead of dwelling on the past and living in defeat, choose to focus on his promises because God wants to restore everything that has been stolen from your life. He wants to restore your joy, your peace, your health, and your finances.*
>
> *You must get your hopes up and decide to get your thoughts and words going in the right direction. Today, choose to focus on the future and release past hurts through forgiveness. Draw a line in the sand and say, "I am a child of the Most High God, and*

I am not going to live my life negative and defeated. This is a new day, and I am taking back what belongs to me!

(unknown)

PART TWO

The Spirit of My Heart Speaks

*I am the **eighth** of ten **core** children born to Chester and Ruth Nelson. I was raised with both parents in the home. I witnessed my father as the only provider and my mother as the nurturer and prayer warrior. Children are basically an extension of their socialization. The core beliefs value I saw were providing, nurturing and praying. I was young when my father passed away; however, my father obviously trained my brothers to take up any lack or slack. I am 5 years older than my younger brother and 3 years older than my baby sister. Five plus three is eight. I believe the number **8** has great significance in my life. My younger sister, brother and I, never really wanted or missed out on anything. My parents instilled in us the value of family which still exists today. Dysfunction and all! My mother used to say" **teeth and tongue fall out, but they are still a part of the mouth**" I did* *not understand fully what she was saying, but we her children, thought it was cute. Later, I realized she was telling us no matter what, we were to band together.*

I remember my family always happy, laughing, singing, playing, fellowshipping with each other until life happened!

*Due to the military, two of my brothers, had already crossed over into what we called the land of Canaan (**California**). I scouted out California in 1972. The remainder of my family relocated to California from St. Louis, Mo. in 1974. In 1976, one of my brothers was brutally murdered. I watched my mother's spirit literally leave her body. My mom's joy left, she smiled less, and her laughter was gone. I wondered what was so powerful to take these precious intangibles away from her. This was my first vivid memory of death and I was traumatized! My brother's death sent my entire family into shock. This death stood out to me because of my mother. My mother's eyes no longer matched her smile. She quietly shut down (desensitized) until God called her home. Money could not reverse or bring my brother back. I also learned to reconcile the trauma of sickness and death by detaching myself and ultimately becoming desensitized. If I did not feel it, I did not have to address it. The pain was so great it immobilized and put me in a **suspended state of pause.** The pain was real! I am an extension of my mother and thus my actions imitated what*

I saw. Let me just say, I have experienced the loss of parents, siblings and husband, but never the loss of a child. My senses tell me it is a different type of pain based upon the look in my mom's eyes. My brother's murder was my first traumatic shock. I had no words for it, yet I could see the pain in my mom's eyes. It was a pain only God could address. I had no idea this death thing would continue until only two ***core*** *siblings left. I use the word* ***core*** *to identify the huge number of family members from the original vine. I lose count to all the cousins, nieces, nephews, grandchildren, and great grandchildren that are branches from the* ***core****!*

My heart houses the real me, the seat of my character and affections. Lodged inside my heart was trauma, grief, hurt, and fear. These emotions were neatly tucked away until sickness and death forced me to examine myself.

. Pastor Hunter teaches us all the time that ***Prayer*** *is the* ***antidote*** *for fear.* ***(Philippians 4:6 KJV)*** *tells us to be anxious for nothing* ***(Do Not Worry)****, but in everything with prayer and supplication with thanksgiving, make our request known to God. Pray about everything, with thankfulness to God. The peace of God is waiting to guard our hearts and mind through Christ Jesus.*

In preparation of my brother's wake and funeral services, I learned and witnessed a ***grieving protocol*** *if you will. There were words of encouragement, food, and financial acts of kindness shown to my family. I learned during grieving time****; people simply need to know you are there****. Bereavement is a time to utilize your talent of kindness. It is needed and greatly appreciated. Allow the bereaved to speak first if there be any speaking; remember you are only there for support. My mother was never much of a talker unless it was with her sister (****Aunt Jessie****). They had such a bond and it was such a joy to see them together. The bond they had was short of miraculous. My mother only wanted her son back, not to answer when, where, and how! Remember, your presence speaks volumes.*

The Spirit of My Heart Speaks

Trauma *taught me to push myself and put my game face on faithfully go to work, church and about my normal routine, only in a semi-fog. I also learned that I am both my mother and my father. My mother's character was gentle and loving, but my father was* ***no nonsense****. I am a mixture of both and more of one depending upon the situation. Core Belief System! I was taught by my mother to believe the word of God for my life. I trusted the word of God all while holding my breath.* ***Grief*** *is a matter* *of the heart, such heaviness which I learned how to mask so well.* ***Deep down in my heart were all these feeling and emotions with nowhere to go!***

There have been so many dangers seen and unseen in my life where God kept me. I am convinced that God has a divine purpose for my life. The number eight! I believe without a doubt that if it had not been for God, who was on my side, where would I be? I learned that God is Sovereign (encompassing all space and time); he can handle any question, doubt or fears I may have. I learned to tap into his glory through applying his word. It gives me such joy to have his word as my ***lifeline*** *to him.*

My second mind blowing ***trauma*** *came when my mother was diagnosed with stage four colon cancer. At this point I am thinking* ***God, what are you doing?*** *I am not happy to say I was angry with God and my family. How could this be? My brother and I were taking turns accompanying my mother to her doctor's appointments. The doctor never consulted or asked permission to take my breath away with this diagnosis. Why now, he never mentioned it before. The statement that put my mind in a tailspin was when the doctor told us my mother had about six months (****which turned out to be six weeks****). He then said she, my mother,* ***had reached her longevity****. What in the Heaven! Was that supposed to be comforting? My emotional* *beast was ready to put the paws on him! I thought that statement was so disrespectful and unprofessional. I lost it! I was not able to sue him, but if I saw him today, I might just bump into him on purpose, accidently! I got his longevity! More t***rauma***, ***grief*** *and* ***hurt*** *to deal with! I turned my dining room into a hospice, and we took shifts caring for my mother. My mother was transitioning faster than the original time frame given to us, so she was admitted into hospice; she immediately went to be with GOD.*

Part Two**: **The Spirit of My Heart Speaks

I learned when you walk through sickness and death with your love ones, it helps you with closure. It still hurts, but such peace knowing she is not in pain anymore! You need closure to reconcile your emotions.

Death taught me, you can have all the money in the world and simply exist! Existing is no fun! I partially held my breath for so long until it ***took breast cancer to force me to breath*** *and live life to the fullest. I wanted to live! I wanted to be a better version of me! I do not have the energy to worry about how I am going to pay this one or that one;* ***I have learned to trust God for that!*** *Money is just a tool to assist and enable us to live better, help* others and support the ministry. God has met every expectation I ever placed at his feet and some! **Overflow!**

You cannot beg, borrow, or steal good health. I realized sickness and death was a tool for my ministry and God was schooling me on the task ahead. My job was to encourage, support, and be care-giver for my family spiritually and financially. Well needless to say, from 1993 to 2012, there was a tsunami of sickness, disease, and death in my family including myself. My love for my family over-ruled the anger and resentment I felt towards some of them. I blamed some of my family members for my mother's death. I knew it was cancer, but I felt everyone did not share fully in the responsibility to save her. **I wanted to save her!** Forget the doctor, I felt if we all banded and prayed together, we could save her. I was angry that my siblings did not feel the same way I did. You only get one mother and she should have been treated like a queen on all cylinders. **Bishop Humphrey** told me when my husband passed that everyone grieves differently, and I needed to accept their feelings. **God upheld me with his right hand** and My Pastor said one morning on the prayer line that **God remembers**. This sent shock waves through my entire body down to my **core.** Instantly, it addressed the trauma I had experienced. I did not see it coming nor was I ready for what happened on the prayer line that morning. God allowed the trauma, and pain to cause me to trust him more and more, while he purged the residue *anger and un-forgiveness from my heart.* ***He remembered to uphold me!*** *It was if God himself was personally telling me I remember what you have endured through the voice of my Pastor.*

Part Two: The Spirit of my Heart Speaks

Eventually, my anger towards some of my family subsided. The more I poured out to God, the more God released my anger and un-forgiveness. As I trusted him more, it became easier to forgive. I am not proud of this, but my temper was a force to be reckoned with. ***I have learned over time not to personalize things because if people really knew what they were up against, would they even think to bother you****? I reason very well with myself! Thank you, Lord, for the control of self! I am so thankful to experience the goodness of the Lord while in the land of the living. I thank God for being a Keeper!* ***My Keeper!*** *After all, I am only responsible for my actions. My tears are the purge of all the trauma and sorrow I have witnessed. God gave me a revelation through his word and now I dine on the word. God gave me a release! My praise is tears of joy, and my worship then shows up as thank you laughter in the spirit! Crying and laughing at the same time.* ***I still do not quite understand this, but I thank God for it.***

I Got my Happy Back! Yes, I Got my Happy Back!

There is more work to be done for the trauma I have experience, but I believe God for a total release of any residue hurt, grief, or un-forgiveness. Acknowledgement is the first key to freedom! I am convinced, it is impossible to be a good steward with Spiritual and Emotional Baggage. Spiritual and Emotional Baggage clogs your mind, cripples your thinking and stops your forward movement.

The death of my mother still hurts to this day. She wore several hats for me, mother, friend and confidant. I have such peace knowing that God chose her to be my mother and she loved us to the end.

Experience, Grace and Peace showed up when my husband was diagnosed with brain cancer. Time was moving at warped speed. Home Hospice extended his quality of life allowing him to die with dignity. Watching my mom, brother, and now my husband battle cancer, rekindled my anger. The word of God was all I had to keep me going. ***I was confused at how I could trust God and be angry with him at the same time****. When I reflect on those times, I feel so sad because God has truly blessed me beyond measures. I realized later; God can handle anything I brought to him. Thus, he is GOD!*

<u>Part Two</u>: The Spirit of my Heart Speaks

Cancer seemed to attack my family all over the globe. One cancer diagnosis after the other! One by one cancer was knocking us down like bowling pins. Cancer is maternal and paternal in my family line.

I needed to know why?????? I was still alive!

I first heard this phrase in one of DB Bedford's I Never Worry seminars. ***FEAR is False Evidence Appearing Real.*** *Fear maybe be false, but it was a powerful spirit that overwhelmed me! You cannot successfully accomplish anything operating under the pressure of fear. I needed to address the fear because God did not give us a spirit of fear, but of power, love, and a sound mind. My fear was* ***UN-BE-LIVE-ABLE!*** *I just knew I would be next. I would whisper in my husband's ear and tell him to"* ***<u>fight for your life",</u>*** *he would smile and say, "I'm fighting." We prayed his favorite scripture (**Proverbs_3:4-5 KJV)** Trust in the Lord with all your heart, lean not unto your own understanding, in all thy ways acknowledge him and he will direct thy paths. This scripture spoke to him as we prayed it, over and over! Being a caretaker is not an easy task. I faced many challenges at work during this time. I had put my game face on, went in to work and come home to watch my husband slowly die. He did get to* *see our baby girl graduate from College before he closed his eyes for the last time. I commend all those with hearts to work within Hospice Situations. It is a beautiful thing to place another's health and well-being before your own. It is so important to be mindful of how we treat people* ***<u>you never know what a person is dealing with</u>*** *daily.*

I Never Worry Platform is deeply rooted in the word of God. ***<u>Galatians 5:22</u>*** *the Fruits of the Spirit.* ***Intangible things are virtues that money cannot buy.*** *If you ever get an opportunity to experience one of his seminars, the fruits of the spirits will immediately come to mind.*

PART THREE

SPECIAL INSERTION

JESUS, CANCER AND ME

If it were up to me, I would have taken this information to the grave with me. The Holy Spirit moved me to share and prayerfully bless someone else. ***September 26, 1998*** *a lump was removed from my right breast. Sovereign God personally showed me he was* ***Bigger*** *than cancer. I was diagnosed with an overly aggressive form of breast cancer. I hung up on my doctor, went into my bedroom, where I sat down on the floor and cried and prayed, prayed and cried for three days. I had to do this in stealth motion as I did not want my family to fall apart at the news. I did not tell them, initially. I cannot remember when I told them; maybe they saw me crying I do not remember. What I do remember is the Holy Spirit whispered to me and said this is* ***not unto death****. God remembers you and will uphold you with his right hand! I got up showered, brushed my teeth and* *called my doctor back and inquired on his plan of action. I looked up the number* ***8*** *out of curiosity and found that the number* ***8*** *represents a new order, new beginning, a symbol related to constant energy flow and power. It is also related to wealth and power. The biblical definition that stuck out to me was the number* ***8*** *symbolized* ***man's true born-again event, when he was resurrected from death to life.*** *I treasured this definition because I believed I was the next one to face death in my family, only to find out this cancer was not unto death. I was given a new chance at life! I have yet to find words in the dictionary to describe my feelings. Hallelujah, Oh God; Thank you, Oh God! Oh God Bless your Holy name is all I seem to be able to say before the monsoon of tears come!*

"Not unto Death" *kept ringing in my ears. My diagnosis turned out to be such a blessing. Cancer demanded me to utilize my time and my talents. The blessing of my experience with cancer was three scriptures given to me and I planted them deep, deep, deep, down in my spirit. I placed them to my memory until they became soft knowledge. I needed something to eradicate my fear from the root. I used those scriptures to address my fear while I trusted God to heal me. God is all I have, so if I were to be healed,* ***God*** *would have to do it! Grief, anger, and fear were my bottled-up emotions that found their release through cancer. I am deeply passionate about many things, but I needed the spirit of* *my emotions to align to the word of God. I share these scriptures with all God sends my way.*

I know the Lord can do it all at once, but there were some things I needed to release before the healing process began. My healing process came in phases. God allowed me to watch myself and journal my feelings as he walked me through the process of breast cancer. My village of family, co-workers, and church members were supportive in agreement with my healing. The Prayers of the righteous avails much! I felt the prayers and I believe those prayers are the catalyst that keeps my mind and spirit going to this day. I would like to refer this phase as my mental healing. Immediately, I had to adjust my mind to a new normal. This is where my faith aligned with the will of God. My ordeal with cancer taught me to totally trust and depend upon the word of God.

My priorities are more focused on what ***God wants*** *to do with my life and not what* <u>*self-sufficient Carolyn*</u> *thought she could do. October 21, 1998 brought my physical phase of healing. I had a lumpectomy and thirty-three lymph nodes removed. All returned negative, the cancer had not spread. I consider myself a wordsmith; however, all the words I know cannot fully describe how thankful I was to hear those words. My heart does not fully understand why I was chosen to live after so many of my family members lost their battle with cancer, diabetes, renal failure and* *congestive heart failure. I just remind myself of the number* ***8****, my born-again re-birth. I cherish the vision I have of meeting Jesus where we are skipping rocks together, it makes my heart happy! My assignment is not up, and God has more work for me to do.*

PART THREE: SPECIAL INSERTION

The next course of action would be four, twenty-one-day cycles of chemo and thirty-three treatments of radiation. ***Psalms 27*** *was my prayer for chemo; the Lord is my light and my salvation of whom shall, I fear? The Lord is the strength of my life of whom shall I be afraid? When my enemy (cancer) and my foe (fear of cancer) came against me to eat up my flesh, it stumbled and fell.*

Why?

Because he was wounded for my transgressions, bruised for my iniquities, the price of my peace was upon him, and with his stripes I am healed. My salvation was settled at the cross.

Why?

Because the Lord is my shepherd and I shall not want … yes, I might walk through the valley of the shadow of death, but his rod and staff comfort me. He prepares a table before me in the presence of my enemy (cancer) surely goodness and mercy shall follow me all the days of my life and I will dwell in the house of the Lord forever. Amen! It gives me great comfort when I join several scriptures together. The word is like a cleansing agent removing negative thoughts and emotions. The word gave me so many things to be thankful for. I only focused s on the out of body experience God had allowed me to witness. I walked alongside myself through the process of cancer. I was in unfamiliar territory! To this day, I can only share so much of this story, I am sharing what I can.

My ***first*** *chemo treatment went well, despite all the information I tried to absorb. I wanted to be pro-active in my healing. Sometimes knowledge can be extremely dangerous when you are unable to put it into context.* ***Pastor Humphrey*** *spoke about* ***information without inspiration and revelation without illumination****. God did not need my help. I did not possess the wisdom to fully understand what was happening. The intravenous drip took five pokes before we could get a vein to work. As the poisons were infiltrating my body, my mind rehearsed* ***Psalms 27****. The side-effects caused sheer exhaustion and severe indigestion. My hair began to shed, so to buffer the blow of losing it all at once, I had my daughter cut my hair short. My* ***second*** *chemo treatment consisted of only three pokes before we got a vein. I began to pick up weight, totally opposite to the stories I heard about cancer patients losing weight. One* *of my biggest fears of chemo was vomiting, something I am truly paranoid of to this day. My* ***third*** *treatment began with nausea, vomiting, and passing out. This episode truly spooked my family. The only thing I remember is running to the bathroom not to throw up on the carpet. I was told I hit my head on the bathroom door and passed out, still vomiting. I could hear in the faint distance my daughter screaming to the top of her lungs, which brought me back. When I regained consciousness; I was surrounded by paramedics. I thank God for giving Tamara such powerful lungs! My neighbors tell me she was outside of the house screaming up and down the street.*

My doctor informed me I was dehydrated, not enough food or liquids in my system to fight the chemo. Needless, to say I will have more than enough of both before the last and final chemo. More pounds! My final chemo treatment came with yet another surprise, I was unable to receive the chemo due to my blood count being too low. I needed to rest and allow my blood platelets to build back up. I started this journey 110 pounds soaking wet, now I am forty pounds heavier and my white blood cells cannot fight for me. My sister friends brought me ***unfermented beet juice****,* ***immune booster****s, and* ***flaxseeds****. We believed this would aid my platelets to return normal.* ***It did!*** *God is a keeper and he does not make mistakes.*

Hallelujah! Final chemo took place on ***February 10, 1999.*** *It took longer to recover from the final treatment, but I have never been more ready to be done with chemo. The only side effects were more exhaustion and dizziness.*

Radiation began ***March 9th, 1999****, so far so good. I am now working twenty hours a week; hoping to bring some normalcy back into my life. Radiation will be thirty-three treatments everyday if I do not miss a treatment. The side effects caused by radiation are burning of the skin to the affected area. Radiation would cross a section of my lungs and the sheer exhaustion.*

It was not until the completion of all treatment when I began to feel anger rearing its ugly head. I needed to understand why? I needed to understand my new mindset. I listed every treatment, every reaction, every response, and every surgery. For some strange reason, the fear was gone. I looked for it, expected it to pop up at any moment, but it did not. I read up on breast cancer to the point of holding legitimate conversations with my oncologists. I believed I majored in medicine!

PART THREE: SPECIAL INSCERTION

I gave my first testimony, only to walk away convinced this was why God kept me alive. I later found another reason why God is keeping me. Not only do I speak about it, I am about it!

My ***first*** *experience with cancer was to enhance or deepen my personal relationship God and what he can do. I no longer needed to reference my mother's Jesus or speak in the third person. In addition to my mother's or husband experience, I now have my very own up close and personal experience. My first experience addressed my fears, my why me. God needed me to know that he did not give me a spirit of fear, but of power, love, and a sound mind. He needed me to understand that he was the* ***God over everything, even cancer.*** *Even My fear! God proved this by allowing me to watch myself go through it. The word cancer is very threatening, extremely scary and always a reminder of death for me. In addressing the fear, it gave me the tools to encourage others assigned to me. I understand when someone says they are fearful. I really understand!* ***My second experience was for others!*** *Encouraging them to stand on God's word believing that his word does not come back to him empty but accomplishes what he sent it to do. I can humbly walk down the runway with* ***all the survivors*** *in preparation to share with the next man, women, boy or girl that* ***GOD*** *is bigger than cancer! I not only have a* *testimony;* ***I AM A TESTIMONY!*** *The choir sings:" I may have some scars, I am healed, disappointments, I'm still healed!*

Cancer has no respect for ***money, title,*** *or* ***position****. Money means nothing to illness. Illness is an equal opportunist! Sickness will help you to put money in its proper perspective, as the link between the means and the end. Sickness will also let you know who* ***really*** *is in charge. My advice to all women is do your breast self-examinations, get your mammograms; early detections can save your life. Healthy diet and exercise will strengthen your immune system. Medicine is more advanced now than it was during my experience. More reason to be on top of your health!*

PART THREE: SPECIAL INSCERTION

Fast forward: ***2012*** *I lost two more family members, leaving only my younger brother and myself.* ***14 years of remission*** *and the cancer returns to the same breast. The story I am telling myself is* ***countless biopsies****, many* ***surgeries,*** *months of* ***chemo*** *and* ***thirty-three treatments of radiation*** *and the cancer comes back! My vision in the natural was exchanged with the spiritual. Radiation crossed my lungs and now there is asthma. Tension alopecia, and skin issues. I can go on and on about how cancer has altered my body, but*

I'M STILL HERE! *My spirit sings "I've had some good days," I've had some hills to climb;" I have had some weary days and some sleepless nights. But when I look around and I think things over, all my good days outweigh my bad days and I will not complain. Sometimes the clouds hang low and I can hardly see the road. I ask the question 'Why so much pain?' But God knows what is best for me, my weary eyes cannot see. I will just say thank you Lord, I will not complain. Why? God has been good to me, he has been so good to me, more than this cruel world could ever be he has been good to me. He dried all my tears away, turned my midnight into day, I will just say thank you Lord, I will not complain!*

The things that went wrong cannot compare to the fact that I am still here! Cancer was relentless; but God's purpose for my life was more relentless. God's purpose prevailed!

My Scripture Mantras:

Before each surgery, **Psalms 23** *was my kickoff. I called on* **Psalms 27**, *after I regained consciousness. Both scriptures ministered to me as the poisonous drip was going through my body killing both cancerous and healthy cells. Every beam of radiation sent through my body was sealed with these scriptures.*

PART THREE: SPECIAL INSERTION

*. My obedience blessed me to understand and apply the principle of sowing into the kingdom. My spiritual stewardship allowed me to share some of my story. One of God's many titles is **Jehovah RAAH!** The shepherd, who leads and guides us.*

*The Lord is my shepherd and I shall not want **(provision**). He makes me lie down in green pastures, (**rest**) he leads me besides the still waters **(peace**). God covered me like a canopy. I believe this and expect God to supply all my needs, not because I am so good, but because God is not a man that he should lie, neither the son of man that he should repent. If God said it, that settles it for me. The Psalmist says God will prepare a table for me in the presence of my enemies. Imagine your table spread with all your favorite foods and decorated with no sorrows, no health issues, no troubled marriages, no money woes, and the tablecloth laced with the fruits of the spirit. The shepherd has covered everything. Finally, he sends goodness and mercy to follow us. As vivid as my imagination is, I cannot make this up.*

Read it for yourself!

***March 2020.** My oldest daughter found a knot in her left breast which turned out to be breast cancer. Charity begins at home and* *spreads abroad. This news confirmed the why I had to go through what I went through to minister to my child. There is a marked difference between watching someone else battle an illness and you, yourself battling that same illness. My daughter's mantra is that cancer only attacked her body, not her mind, heart or spirit. I am thankful she can speak this over herself. I will allow her to give you details in her own book.*

*We are currently in this process of surgery, chemo, and radiation. I believe that my daughter will be fine and come out with such a testimony of encouragement to younger women. Initially, I was concerned because of the pandemic covid 2019, but I realized that God himself was speaking to the entire world. Pastor Hunter teaches us on Psalms 46. (**Psalms 46:10 KJV**) tells us to **be still and know that he is God, God will be exalted among the heathens (unbelievers) and he will be exalted in the earth.***

I find this so comforting because all strong holds, chains, titles, positions, money, cars, houses, tissue and Clorox wipes mean absolutely nothing at this time of quarantine. I believe the sooner we all come to acknowledge him as the supreme omnipotent God that he is, the virus will self-destruct.

Speak this to the covid.2019 virus and anyone you may know that tested positive. Psalms 27: The Lord is my light

and my salvation of whom shall, I fear? The Lord is the strength of my life who shall I be afraid? When the wicked, even mine enemies, and my foes came upon me to eat up my flesh, they stumbled and fell.

PART FOUR

MONEY

Thus far I have discussed two of the three components in removing the curse of poverty in your life. The Mind and Heart. The third component is ***money*** *and my stewardship over money. You often hear people say they are on their grind. What is your grind? For me, my grind was likened to the tale of who ate my cheese. The redundancy of going through the motion everyday believing you are doing the right thing and still ending up in the same place. I reviewed my budget over and over making sure I was following the scrip and yet I continued to come up short. Awesome salary and benefits, yet I was living from paycheck to paycheck. I could not quite figure out what I was missing until I received the words in (****Malachi, chapter 3****KJV) I am not sure who directed me to this book or when, but I am so grateful to them. I learned to apply the word of God to my Finances. I learned there is a direct relationship between how I manage money and the quality of my* *spiritual life. How I managed worldly wealth would determine how much God could trust me with spiritual blessings (true riches). Lifeline of God through his word! Removing the curse of poverty required me to change my mind, examine my heart, and my finances. All three must be aligned and in obedience with the word of God. No, I am not rich by this world's standard! Neither Am I poor by this world's standard? I live in the* ***Blessed Mode of Peace****! I am not sure the cost of peace, but I am positive I could not afford it. God's perfect peace that surpasses all understanding is where I am striving to stay. No need to own shares of stock or grasp after the wind when it all comes from God.*

(Malachi 3, verse 10b KJV) *challenges us to* ***test, try*** *and* ***prove*** *God in our Finances and watch how he honors his word. Wow! I like a challenge, so I tried him, and he has blessed me in accordance to my ability, my skill level, my maturity and the faith that he has given to me. And You! I like the phrase* ***according to his ability in the Parable of the Talents because it speaks individually****. I may not possess the ability to handle the wealth of a celebrity or athlete, so I do not hate, or strive to compete, I congratulate. I know of whom and where that ability comes.*

*My Pastor, (****Gregory D. Hunter, Olivet Oakland****) is also a musician. He can teach, exhort, and play instruments. I can hear music and most times carry a note, but I am unable to play* *or read music. Why, I was not wired and never had a desire to do so. We each are blessed according to our God-given ability specifically when we utilize those abilities. The scripture support and show that God uses finances to teach us to trust him, and for many of us money is the greatest challenge of all. Removing the Curse of Poverty is a process clearly connected to our obedience to the word of God.*

*My favorite part of **Malachi 3** was God rebuking the devourer. I thought to myself, I need God to rebuke the devourer for me because you are blessing me with enough funds only to struggle. That does not make sense to me. I began to review and consider my ways and realized I needed to change my mindset. I removed the X and Y factor, no more unknowns, no more algebraic equations. I now operate in the mindset that God blesses me to get wealth and without him, I can do nothing. I mean absolutely nothing. A robber is up close invading your personal space, where as a thief is sneaky and behind the scenes. The question in Malachi asks" **will a man rob God?"** when I don't give the Lord's tithe, I am robbing him. I do not know about you, but I am not a robber and certainly not a thief. It is almost like one of my daughters, stealing from their own legacy. A tenth is simply a dime on every dollar. I give ten percent and get to be a good steward over the ninety. Tithing gives joy with benefits. Uncle Sam on the other hand, takes and then there is the **period**!*

Money is only a means to an end; it is not the means, nor the end, but the link in between. I had to keep in mind who blessed me with the ability to obtain wealth. We can easily become money driven if we removed God. Remembering I can do nothing without God keeps me humble.

*Come with me to (**Galatians 5:22** KJV) Intangibles are those items money cannot buy. Money cannot buy the fruits of the spirit, we must incorporate them in our daily living, saturate our spirits with them. We must practice Love, Joy, Kindness, Patience, Temperance etc. We incorporate fruits of the spirit by reading, studying, and applying the word of God to our lives.* ***Why would God trust me with more when I have not mastered less?***

I would not give my eleven-year-old grandson the keys to my car and send him on an errand. That would be irresponsible and somewhat ignorant of me. Our Obedience blesses us to acquire more. Our fruit grows in proportion to our ***Obedience to the word of God.*** *Blessings began to come from various places, places you never expected, because the wealth of the wicked is stored up for the righteous. Oftentimes we look for a return from those we pour into, but it always comes back from a different source.*

Remember, a close mouth cannot be fed ***nor*** *can a closed hand receive. (**Ephesians 3:20** KJV) Exceedingly and abundantly most of us have acquired more than our parents, and grandparents could ever imagine. We are blessed to live out some of their secret, silent prayers and the spirit of their dreams! Gods passed that entrepreneurial spirit seed down from Adam to us. God told Adam to take dominion over the earth (**Genesis 1:28**) My living is made by what I am blessed to earn; but I leave my* ***LEGACY*** *by what I* ***give****!*

Time *is one thing we have no control over. Only God knows the time or life of a thing. We must make the best of our time while we are here on this earth. The* ***"negative now"*** *forces us to focus on all we do not have or cannot do or see. It is overwhelming to control your thoughts regarding the lack you may face. The lack is real! So real we are persuaded to find relief.*

This system, as we know it, is not designed for all to advance. The political climate fosters fear among its citizens and we are bombarded by our ***isms*** *and* ***biases.*** *Distractions perpetuate our biases and we continue to be divided. Presently, the world is on quarantine with the Covid.2019 pandemic. The good news is* ***God is still****, yet in control! Please hear me on this, God is still in control and those who place their hope and trust in him are at peace no matter what the distraction.*

Citizens and Government Officials of the United States of America need only ask God for forgiveness; God will hear, and this virus will dissipate. Forgiveness for what you might ask. Forgiveness for not applying Galatians 5:22 towards one another. Forgiveness for taking God and his many blessings for granted.

*Oftentimes we choose the most convenient "**<u>here and now</u>**" which turns out to be a band aid that plunges us deeper into an abyss with varying negative consequences. Negative consequences lead to a cycle of more debt, poverty, jail, drugs, etc. etc. I offer a different thought on how to manage and maximize your time. I heard a story regarding fish, and I am paraphrasing. If I give you a fish, you can eat for a day; but if I teach you how to fish, you can eat for a lifetime.*

*<u>Teaching</u> and <u>educating</u> moves us from dependency and despair to **empowerment!** Teaching removes the victimization mentality to an **elevated determination**! A free mind is awesome, no worry, no stress, and no anxiety. Spending time with your loved ones is a character-building trait that will go on and on down your genealogical line.*

Now let us start connecting the three components together.

*<u>**Tithe**</u> is a tenth of your gross earnings, one dime on a dollar. The tithe is what we owe God. On the other hand, Uncle Sam took*

his percentage of my gross bi-weekly income whether I liked it or not. If for some reason I do not pay enough into this system, I will owe at the end of the year. Once again, this is the law of the land and as a citizen, I must obey the law. Therefore: I have no excuse ***not*** *to give the Lord his tithe.*

It was Jehovah- Jirah (our provider) that blessed me to keep my head above water, and I do not swim! I still have days where my mind struggles, but when I go against the principle, my mind does not rest, my spirit struggles for peace and quiet. And it shows up in my finances. My need to ***control*** *is daily dying and manifesting itself into a desire to trust God more and more.*

Has this ever happened to you?

It is Monday, you have a quarter tank of gas that must last for seven days until you get paid. My husband always admonished me to keep at least half tank of gas in my car in case of a sudden emergency. The refrigerator is a little light on food, you forgot to pay a bill, your house was broken into, the car needs new brakes, tuition is due. The doctor says the x-ray shows cancer. What do you do? I laid all of these on the altar in prayer and God shut the devourer down, he opened the windows of heaven and poured out blessings with overflow, leftovers. Due to my obedience in tithing, what the devil meant for evil God turned those things to work in my favor. It did not happen by osmosis, but by standing on his word. "I'm saying that when you are obedient to the word of God, he not only speaks, but he moves to action. I was always told action speaks louder than words. ***God is Love in Action!***

We each have experienced and graduated several tests and trials in our lives. Those test and trials give us the needed testimony to empower and encourage someone else. I believe each of us have people assigned to us to be blessed by the trials and test we ourselves have overcome. People are our greatest investment. ***(Love your neighbor as yourself)*** *The sooner we complete one assignment, the sooner we can move on to the next person in line. My desire is not to keep those assigned to me waiting in line because I am stuck. If I am stuck, it will delay their deliverance, or break through. My tests, your tests, have now become your testimony. My mess, your mess is the essence of your message that someone desperately needs to hear!*

*The life changing word or deed I need to deposit can make the difference if someone lives or dies. The word of faith is nigh in your mouth, in my mouth. Earlier, I mentioned money is only the link between the means and the end, so I am not impressed by money (****anymore****), social status or job title. You get my attention based upon how you treat people.* ***I am impressed by the way we treat each other.*** *Our treatment of others speaks volumes* *to who we are, speaks louder than where you live, the type of car we drive, or the clothes we wear. Poor treatment of each other hinders us from ministering to those assigned to us. Spending time and sharing whatever you have, a word or a hug goes a long way. It is also an excellent way to utilize both your* ***time*** *and your* ***talent****. Just know that* ***<u>each one of us is the answer to someone's prayer.</u>***

PART FIVE

APPLICATIONS

CHALLENGE #1

Close your eyes and envision where you wish to be in five years, ten years (you must have a vision or a plan) Envision what it is you hope to accomplish (you were wired to have goals and dreams) Where are you financially? (God's plans are to prosper you) Envision yourself fulfilling the purpose God had in mind when he created you. (Be fruitful and multiply), have dominion over the earth. If you are not sure what it is, you should be doing simply ask God. What should I be doing?

Can you see yourself?

Are you where you want to be?

Do you need to adjust?

If not, let us look at our Finances and view tools that can assist us in reaching those goals.

***I** will introduce and offer some basic financial tools to assist you in removing the curse of poverty from your life and becoming a better steward over what you have.*

***Budget**: shows you where you are and what you are doing with your money at a specific point in time.*

A budget is simple spending plan or an itemized account of how money comes in, and how it goes out. A budget allows you to get a handle on the flow of your money. Information provided by a budget aids us in making intelligent spending choices. Keeping good financial record allows you to chart your growth.

Most rely on Computer Software programs to keep their budget and balance sheets; however, these programs do not capture the flow of cash. If you do not save every receipt of items you pay with cash, you can only estimate the flow of your cash.

CHALLENGE #2

Sample Budget Plan

<u>FIXED INCOME</u> = $10,000.00 per month

Checking Account #1 <u>Variable Household Expenses</u>

Lord's Tithe	***$1000.00***
Gas	***200.00***
Utilities	***300.00 (PGE, Water, Garbage)***
Groceries	***200.00***
Regular Savings	***<u>1 000.00</u>***
	$2700.00

Checking Account #2	***<u>Fixed Expenses & Investments</u>***
Car Note	***$400.00***
Rent or Mortgage	***$2500.00***
Insurance	***$500.00(Investment)***
Savings Account	***<u>$1000.00 (Roth or 457)</u>***
	$4400.00

Divide your fixed income in half divided by two different accounts.

- ***A.) Monthly Variable expenses paid from this account***
- ***B.) Fixed Expenses and Investment come from this account***

****Utilize a budget, this assist you to get yourself out of debt and take control of your spending****

CHALLENGE#3

Part Five: Applications

We must change our focus to things that appreciate rather than depreciate. There are varying images of wealth. The image of wealth should not be more important than actual wealth. Ask yourself, is it more expedient to drive a Mercedes and live in an apartment or drive a Toyota and own the apartment complex? Is it more important for our children to wear expensive sneakers and not have life insurance on them? If we are honest with ourselves, we seek and want validation. Think about it, God blessed you to pay your own bills, and you do not have to depend on the Joneses. I read a post that said," ***I saw the Joneses in Walmart and their debit/credit card was declined!*** *So, if the Joneses are not doing well, why would we attempt to follow in their shoes? Why are we drowning in debt trying to keep up with an appearance?*

Personally, I would rather have available spending power when needed than an appearance of wealth. If we are honest with ourselves, we seek and want validation. True validation only comes from God!

What are your thoughts? Write them down.

Basic Accounting Equation

Assets - Liabilities = Owner's Equity

***Assets** equal all the things you are blessed to own. Some of our assets decrease in value while others appreciate.*

***Liabilities** equal all the extra bills we accumulate in addition to our monthly expenses. When our out go is more than our income, we are in debt. Operating in the red, in over your head; living in the un-happy place of paycheck to paycheck. **Debt borrows from your future until you are bankrupt. Debt robs, blurs and hides the future**.*

***Owner's Equity** equals those appreciating assets, property, stocks, government bonds, Roth (IRA) Net Worth.*

(Layman's definition)
What you have
minus what you owe
equals what you have left

**Carolyn had ten apples (asset)*
*she **owed** nine of those apples (liabilities)*
leaving Carolyn with one apple (equity or net worth)

** Carolyn had ten apples (assets)*
*but she **owed** fifteen of those apples, (liabilities)*
that would place Carolyn in debt.

Most of us can identify with the layman's definition of the accounting equation as we perform it daily, weekly, bi-weekly and even monthly in our heads.

*It does not matter where you start; you only need to **START** looking at your finances differently!*

CHALLENGE #4

Principle of Percentages

Removing the Curse of Poverty *from our Finances is a process that requires diligence. This principle assisted me in becoming strategic and purposeful with my decision making. I played around with the percentages until I created one that worked for me. Scripture said to write the vision, then make it plain.*

I had to downsize to make my vision plain. I had to decide what was important to me and what I could live without. Out of 100 percent, below is a sample of a living ***structure****. Your percentage can be adjusted to what works for you. My point is the* ***structure*** *piece. Structure your money where it works for you and not against you.*

GIVE *(The Lord's Tithe) Ten Percent*
INVEST *(Insurance; Roth IRA, 457K) Ten Percent*
SAVE *(Twenty Percent or something for the rainy day)*
LIVE *(On or Under) Sixty Percent*

I personally had to start small and work my way to where I desired to be. Baby steps, and once again according to ***your ability.***

Short Term Lowering Debt Goals

Short Term *expenses can be paid off in five years or less and help to reduce debt.* *Once again discipline is the key. You must ask yourself what you are willing to do to secure a debt free future?*

Long Term Debt Lowering Goals

Long Term expenses usually take ten years or more to pay off. Long Term expenses are fixed in nature. These expenses directly affect your credit worthiness with a focus on timeliness of payments.

There are two constants with expenses. Expenses are either ***fixed*** *or* ***variable.*** *The second thing about expenses is you can immediately address the variable ones.* ***Variable Expenses are related to your consumption.*** *Cable offers many channels that we can only watch one at a time. Yes, we are forced (**I feel**) to purchase certain channels we do not want to get some of the channels we* ***do*** *want. Lights are on day and night! Water runs because we like to hear it! We have consumed ourselves into debt. It was a gradual process to get there that will take a mind shift to come out of it.*

CHALLENGE #5

<u>Expenses/Lowering Debt</u>

There are two constants with expenses:

<u>Fixed</u>	***<u>Variable</u>***
Mortgage/Rent	*PGE*
Car Note	*EBMUD*
Insurance (Life, Home, Car)	***Revolving Credit Cards***

One variable expense we shall explore is Revolving Credit. Revolving Credit is alluring and can be deceptive; it does not offer the ability to control the flow of cash or lower debt. ***It subliminally encourages binge spending. Minimum payments*** *are traps to keep you in debt. Minimum payments may address the finance charges, but the principal amount remains closely the same. Being wrapped up in credit card debt does not make a good steward.*

****RUN FROM <u>PAYDAY</u> LOANS, RUN!***

TELL EVERYONE YOU KNOW TO RUN*

Removing the curse of poverty from our Finances requires baby steps. We must reduce and remove unnecessary expenses whenever possible. Yes, there is an uneven distribution of goods and services all over the world. Housing Costs are astronomical (we see tent communities on every other corner) here in America. It grieves my heart that a country big and blessed as the United States has homelessness. I feel there is enough wealth in America to prevent the above types of situations, but I digress. It could be you or me, but for the grace of God. Food is questionable and expensive. Clothing, most of us can give away and still have more than we need. These tools are not answers to the conditions of the world, but insight to getting out of debt.

APPLICATIONS

Becoming the lender and not the borrower!

Let us now explore a few options that can maximize or efforts in lowering debt:

Option #1

Adopt a ***Cash*** *and* ***Carry*** *policy; if you cannot pay cash, carry yourself out of the store.*

Option #2

Set short term goals to pay off all debt, double or triple payments whenever possible. Resolve to only charge the amount you can pay off monthly. This also gives your credit a boost.

Option #3

Request a free copy of your credit report: Transunion, Experian and Equifax. There may be items listed that do not belong to you.

Option #4

Map Out your long-term strategy to pay debt down and then off. The key element to the formula below is you can choose the amount and the time to pay the debt off or down.

Reducing Debt is a process that requires discipline*

Pay Off Amounts	***$5000.00***	***$1000.00***	***$500.00***	***Time Limit***
Divided by 12	*416.67*	*83.34*	*41.67*	*1 year pay off*
Divided by 2	*208.34*			*2 year pay off*
Double Payment		*166.68*	*83.34*	*6-month payoff*

Option#5

Due to identity theft, take caution to your on-line transactions. Occasionally complete a transaction the old way, simply using a pen, paper, and your brain. See if you still have it! It is not the new math!

CHALLENGE #6

Savings Challenge for Men and Women

*Ladies, I know we love to look (**good, fly, on point, lit**) I have been there, done that, and now writing the book. I was a connoisseur of clothes and shoes, and then I grew up. I discovered that comfort best suits me. I discovered that my **personality** brings **life** to whatever I adorn my body with or wear on my foot. Come with me to your closet.*

*First, **we need to pull out every item with the price tag still on it**. Decide if you are going to keep the items, set up a consignment or give them away. If you are like me, you re-arrange your closet before each shopping spree. I found myself purchasing only accessories. I have been buying clothes for years and years and years without enough space to house those items. So, I forget what I already have. I am sure you are guilty of this as well.*

Secondly, we need to sort and arrange clothing items suits, slacks, dresses tops sweaters, coats and finally shoes, bags and accessories.

The challenge** is to arrange and organize clothing items into outfits for each day of the week for thirty days. Utilize every pair of shoes and accessories. Be your very own stylist for 30 days. **If

something hangs idle in your closet, you do not need it*.* *Trust me, by the time you get around to wearing each outfit, you will have saved a considerable amount of money. Of course, the credit card company will increase your limit because they realize you are not spending on the level you once did. Do not be lulled or fooled. Set a spending budget even for shopping. Write yourself a note, it will change your perception of shopping. My younger daughter can roam aimlessly through several stores and come out with nothing. I am a purposeful shopper. I already have in my mind what I want. I see it, purchase it and I am gone. It does not matter the name on the tag, or if the bottom of your shoes is red, white or blue. I am not against designer clothing, but the goal is to remove the curse of poverty.* ***My vanity forced me to do this.*** *I gained so much weight during my battle with cancer I was unable to fit most of my clothes. I traded designer clothes for sweats and pajamas. I remember attending one of my daughter's graduations and her friends did not recognize me because I had on clothes. I was always in my pajamas whenever they came to the house.* ***I needed to lose weight****! I was able to give some away and keep some. I lost the weight. Baby steps! I still wear my pajamas because I love being in my comfort zone.*

What is most important is your spirit when you adorn the outfit. As I mentioned above, your ***personality*** *brings life to whatever you wear. If your* ***heart is right*** *and your* ***body is clean,*** *you* ***<u>are</u>***

on ***"point"*** *in any outfit. The beauty is coming from* ***within****. Think about all the money you will save simply by organizing your closet. Clothing Styles are like a merry-go-round. Styles come and go and come again faster than we realize. Clothing styles are reflective of the eighties as I type.*

Men, I ***challenge*** *you to do the same. Start with your suits, shoes, jeans, sneakers, shirts and ties.*

*Sort and organize your dress shirts, casual shirts. I am sort of envious of the men because it appears that no-matter what they wear, it is always on point. Men can be dressed up with jeans and blazer or a sweat suit. Men can get away with wearing sneakers with a tuxedo. Not women! Nevertheless, follow the same directions given for the women and count your savings. Remember men, it is your "****swag"*** *that brings an outfit to life. There is nothing more attractive than a* ***God fearing****,* ***well-groomed*** *and* ***good smelling man****!*

Hallelujah!

Scripture Lifeline

Challenge Your Mind

<u>Workbook Section</u>

Look up the following scriptures and journal what each scripture means to you. The challenge is two-fold, the words will bless you by committing them to soft knowledge, and you will learn to apply the scripture to your everyday life.

Luke 10:27-28

Matthew 25: 14-40

Deuteronomy 8:18

Malachi 3

Hebrews 11:5-6

Psalms 24:1

Genesis 1-7

Isaiah 55:11

Proverbs 18:21

Psalms 33:9

Galatians 5:22

We must incorporate the word of God within our belief system and our speech; calling those things that are not yet; as if they were.

Scripture Lifeline (King James Version)

(Philippians 4:6-7 KJV) Be anxious for nothing (do not worry) but in everything by prayer petition and thanksgiving present your request to God; and the peace of God which transcends all understanding will guard your heart and minds in Christ Jesus!

(Proverbs 3: 4-5 KJV) Trust in the Lord with thy heart and lean not unto your own understanding; in all thy ways (everything) acknowledge him and he shall direct thy paths.

(Galatians 5:22 KJV) The fruits of the Spirit are love, joy, peace, patience, kindness, goodness, faithfulness, and self-control. These are things where there is no law, intangibles things money cannot buy.

Psalms 23 The Lord is my shepherd, I shall not want, he leads me beside the still waters(peace) … Surely goodness and mercy shall follow me all the days of my life and I will dwell in the house of the Lord forever!

INVESTMENTS:
INSURANCE

I chose whole life insurance for my family as protection and an investment. I am sure it was due to all the sickness and death, I witnessed. I needed to make sure my children were covered. I have witnessed family falling out over money they did not earn. I mean literally not speaking to each for years over money they did not work for yet felt entitled to. I do not wish my children to experience any of what I have witnessed. Although my children do not like having this conversation with me, I am a realist and life happens. So, I encourage everyone to purchase Life Insurance. Purchase whichever one works for you. Whole Life Insurance provides protection if the premiums are paid and can be utilized as an investment after final expenses. Of course, the investment piece depends upon the amount of insurance.

Whole Life Insurance

- *Offers Cash Surrender Value Options (Lowers Debt Benefit of Policy)*
- *Offers Mortgage protection options*

- *Dividends and Annuities Options (additional streams of income)*
- *Offer Rider Options (protection for children under same policy with parents)*

***Everyone needs insurance**! Choose an insurance that suits your need, the point is everyone needs insurance. Insurance aids us in making informed decisions during vulnerable and emotional times in our lives. Insurance alleviates additional debt to loved ones left behind. I am a huge fan of whole life insurance and a burial plan. Certain health issues will prevent you from getting life insurance, but there is always a burial plan inclusive of plots for those family members. My prayer is for everyone to have a minimum of twenty-five thousand dollars for each member of your family.*

Part Five Applications

ICE

*In addition to Insurance, everyone needs ICE. If you do not have a **living will or trust**, **ICE** is the next best thing. Gather the following items and make copies, place in a folder and label its Ice. Secure the folder in case of Emergency.*

I= In

C=Case

E= (of) Emergency

- *Where Insurance Policies are kept*
- *Type of Arrangements*
- *Obituary*
- *Payment of Final Bills*
- *Where, When, How, Who to Contact*
- *Driver's License*
- *Id (if you do not drive)*
- *Social Security Card*
- *All Credits Cards*
- *Update list as needed*

Your list can be as long or short as you desire, just know it will be of great assistance to family members ***In Case of Emergency!***

Olivet members attend the GYM (where we grow our minds in the word) Our Pastor walked us through Psalms 1. I am paraphrasing: The pastor said there is a progression to sin when we walk, stand and sit with the ungodly.

I am using this same scripture to share with you the progression to removing the curse of poverty from your life.

(Blessed) or (Happy) is the man that does not walk in the counsel of the un-godly (taking bad advice from the un-godly); nor stand in the way of sinners; (walking away from God or in the same path of sinners) or sit in the seat with scorners (those who mock or deny God); a Godly man delights in the law (word) of God and meditates on it day and night (builds a relationship through devotion) This man is like a tree planted by the rivers of waters (his roots are constantly receiving nourishment); his leaves yields fruit (at the purposed time) and do not wither; and what so ever he does prospers! Whatsoever he does prosper!

My gift has carried me to places that my knowledge and education could not penetrate.

I have been vulnerable in sharing very personal items of my life. I pray that the Lord and readers are pleased. I chose to follow the Holy Spirit and share in hope that this book will bless someone. My prayer for those who read this book is that the blessings of the Lord overtake you in all aspects of your life. I pray you will be blessed by the renewing of their mind, blessed in you spirt and blessed in your finances. I pray God blesses every place you step and everything your hand touches to prosper in accordance to (Jeremiah 29:11KJV) the plans he has for you before

you were formed in your mother's womb. Plans to prosper you and give you a happy outcome. Of course, this is in conjunction to us playing our part.

I believe God for you and pray you will believe and experience a debt-free life!

The wealth of the wicked is stored up for the righteous!

The seed that leaves your hand will plant itself in your future!

Wherever your mind goes, your will and emotions follow!

God never gives a dream that matches your budget, he is not checking your bank account; God is checking your faith and I quote (TD Jakes)

BE BLESSED!

WORKBOOK:

Review the following terms, adopt, and put it into practice. Take the nouns and make them (transitive verbs) actions words in your life.

Stewardship: is becoming a good steward in managing your time, talent, and tenth.

Basic Accounting Equation: (layman version) what you own minus what you owe, equals owner's equity; financial standing.

Assets: can be property, children, knowledge, money or spiritual gifts.

Liabilities: can be rent, tuition or anything thing you owe

Variable Expenses are those controlled by your usage

Fixed Expenses mortgages, car notes

Can you answer these?

What are the objectives of the book?

What are the three components?

Who owns everything?

Insurance

Investments

Percentage Principle

ICE

TITHING, REMOVES THE CURSE OF POVERTY

PARTING WORDS

This book is dedicated to all those who love the Lord and trust in the word of God for their lives. The lifeeline to God is through his word! I promise all who read this book if you trust in the Lord with whatever you presently have, he will take it and blow on it. Exceedingly and abundantly above anything you can ask or think. ***Removing the curse of Poverty*** *starts in your mind, so change your mind.* ***Romans 12: 2*** *tell us to be transformed by the renewing of or minds! Go to the root of your emotions, acknowledge whatever is in your heart, pray over it and then release it. Life is too short! Examine your heart because whatever is in your heart will manifest itself into your actions. Once your mind is changed and your spirit is free, your outlook and outcome are* ***DIFFERENT****!*

Tithe, Invest, and watch your Finances improve!
Trust God for everything, he can handle it all!
Our minds are powerful, so change your mind!
Release toxicity from the emotions of your heart (fear, anger, jealousy, insecurity) Practice the Fruits of the Spirit
Create and Structure a financial plan and follow it!

The rewards of being Faithful:

Our reward as told in Jeremiah 29:11 says I know the plans of you, plans to prosper you and not harm you, plans to give you hope and a future, says the Lord! The plan includes rebuking the devourer for our sakes. The first two servant final reward was well done thy good and faithful servant! You have been faithful over a few things; I will make you ruler over many things. The first two servants proved themselves as trustworthy, good stewards. Who does not want to hear these words from God? I know I do!

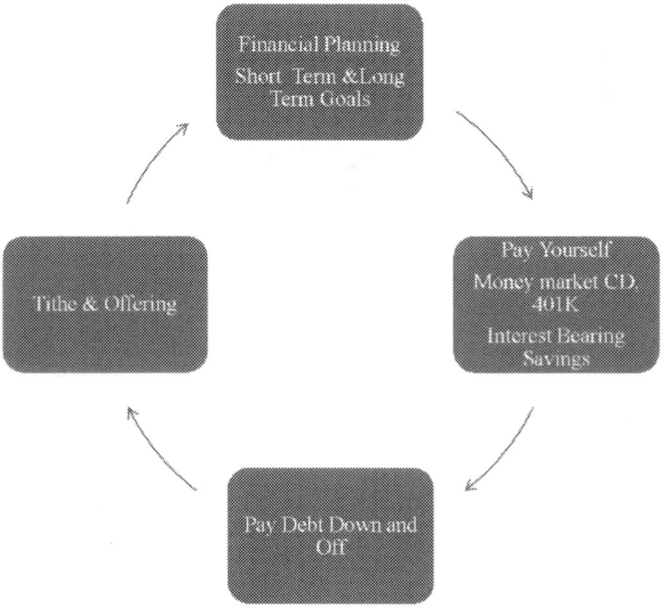
Financial Planning
Short Term &Long Term Goals
Pay Yourself
Money market CD. 401K
Interest Bearing Savings
Pay Debt Down and Off
Tithe & Offering

BORROWED QUOTES:

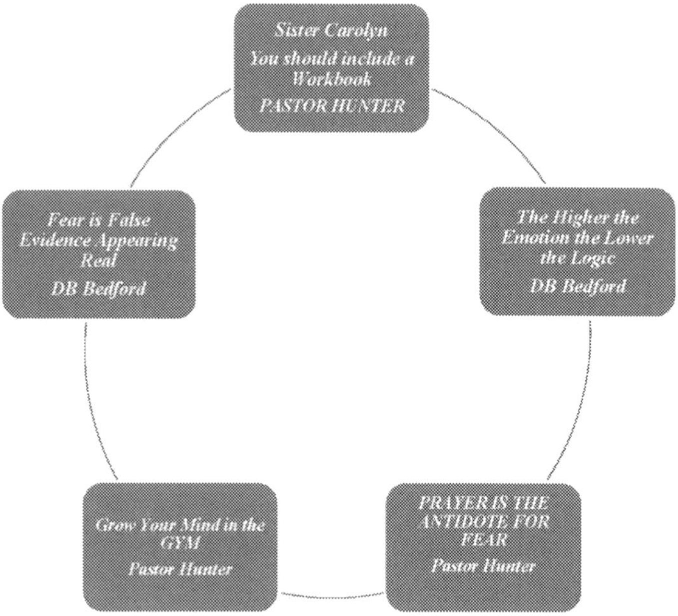

ACKNOWLEDGEMENT

Pastor Gregory D Hunter

Pastor Maurice Bates

DB Bedford, Emotional Intelligence Consultant.

WE CAN'T CHANGE WHAT IS GOING ON AROUND IS UNTIL WE CHANGE WHAT IS GOING ON INSIDE OF US!

Goal is to share tools on removing poverty from the Mindset, Spirit, and Finances.

Printed in the United States
By Bookmasters